DISNEY PRINCESS STORIES

AAHANA TAKALE

ISBN 979-888503353-4

Contents

Mulan

Thousands of years ago in ancient China, there lived a beautiful young woman named Mulan. She lived with her parents and a dog named Little Brother.Mulan's father had once been a great warrior, but his leg had been injured in battle. As an only child, Mulan felt responsible for upholding the family honor.One day, a man arrived with terrible news from the Emperor. The Huns, China's enemy, had invaded.The Emperor had ordered that one man from every family must join the Imperial Army. Mulan's aging father had to fight...again.Mulan knew her father was too old to fight. Late that night, she made a big decision.After saying a prayer to the Ancestors, she used a sword to cut her hair short. Then she put on her father's warrior clothes.

As her parents slept, Mulan, now dressed as a young man, jumped onto her father's horse, Khan.

Then she raced off to join the Imperial Army in her father's place. Somehow, she would find a way to bring honor to her family.When Mulan arrived at the Imperial Army's training camp, she met Captain Li Shang. "What is your name?" he asked Mulan.My name? It's, uh...Ping!" Mulan said. To her amazement, Shang and the other soldiers believed she was a man!Shang worked hard to teach his soldiers strength and discipline. Mulan struggled to keep up. Frustrated, Shang told her to go home.But to earn the soldiers' respect, Mulan retrieved an arrow atop a tall pole. This was the hardest training task of all, and

Mulan had done it!Mulan was not alone on her journey. A dragon named Mushu, sent from the Ancestors to be her guardian, and a cricket named Cri-Kee were always at her side.Working together, they wrote a fake letter ordering Shang and his soldiers to go after the Huns. Now Mulan would get her chance to bring honor to her family.Heeding the letter's message, Shang led his soldiers into the mountains. Suddenly, they were surrounded by thousands of Huns. Mulan got an idea.She grabbed the very last cannon and, using Mushu's flame, lit the fuse. The cannon caused a massive avalanche of snow to fall on the Huns.She grabbed the very last cannon and, using Mushu's flame, lit the fuse. The cannon caused a massive avalanche of snow to fall on the Huns.

But the danger wasn't over. Snow was now racing toward Mulan and her friends.

Mulan's loyal horse, Khan, ran to her side. She jumped onto his back, and just as the snow was about to bury Shang, Mulan pulled him to safety.

During the battle, Mulan had been injured. While caring for her wound, a medic realized that "Ping" was a woman. Shang had no choice but to leave Mulan behind.

As she sat with Khan, Mushu, and Cri-Kee, Mulan felt she had failed her family and herself. Then she heard the Huns' voices.Mulan raced to the Imperial City to warn Shang. "The Huns are alive!" she told him. "They're in the city."But Shang felt betrayed by Mulan and did not trust her. Mulan tried warning the others, but no one would believe her.The Hun leader, Shan-Yu, kidnapped the Emperor, but Mulan and Shang rescued him. Furious, Shan-Yu chased Mulan onto the palace roof - exactly as she planned.

Mulan grabbed Shan-Yu's sword and pinned his coat to the roof. He couldn't move when Mushu and Cri-Kee shot a rocket his way.

The force of the explosion sent Mushu and Cri-Kee flying through the air. Mulan and Shang fell together to the ground as fireworks began to fill the sky.The people were celebrating. The Huns had been banished, and the Imperial City was safe!The Emperor was very grateful to Mulan. "You have saved us all," he said, and then he did something extraordinary: The Emperor bowed to Mulan.Everyone in the plaza bowed to Mulan, too. The Emperor asked her to stay on as his adviser, but Mulan knew it was time to return to her family.At home, Mulan presented her father with a sword given to her by the Emperor."The greatest gift and honor is having you for a daughter," her father said. "I've missed you so.""Excuse me," said a voice behind them. "Does Mulan live here?" Shang had brought Mulan her helmet...and she invited him to stay for dinner.

Rupenzel

Long ago, a king and queen had a baby daughter named Rapunzel.What her devoted parents didn't know was that Rapunzel's golden hair contained magical healing powers.A selfish old woman named Mother Gothel knew of the magic in Rapunzel's hair and wanted it to keep herself young.

So she kidnapped the baby and raised her in a tower deep in the woods, never telling her that she was a princess.As Rapunzel's hair grew and grew, she loved gazing out the tower window at the lights that floated in the night sky every year on her birthday.She longed to leave the tower and see them up close, but Mother Gothel refused.Meanwhile, a young thief named Flynn Rider had stolen something special from the King's castle, and the royal guards were after him.Suddenly, he saw the perfect hiding place—a tower!

When Flynn Rider climbed into the tower, Rapunzel knocked him out with a frying pan.

Then she secretly inspected the satchel he carried. Inside, Rapunzel found a sparkling gold object. It was so familiar.Flynn Rider awoke and found himself tied to a chair with Rapunzel's long, golden hair. Rapunzel pointed to her painting of the floating lights.

Tomorrow was her eighteenth birthday. If Flynn took her to see the lights, she'd return his satchel.

After Flynn agreed to help, Rapunzel used her hair to climb down from the tower.She'd never been outside before! But when her feet touched the grass, Rapunzel nearly burst with excitement, exclaiming, "Woo-hoo!"Rapunzel and Flynn enjoyed their adventure, but they were being chased! Mother Gothel was looking for them.

Rapunzel and Flynn enjoyed their adventure, but they were being chased! Mother Gothel was looking for them.

The royal guards were after Flynn, and so were his angry partners in crime. They wanted the crown!

Rapunzel and Flynn enjoyed their adventure, but they were being chased! Mother Gothel was looking for them.

The royal guards were after Flynn, and so were his angry partners in crime. They wanted the crown!One morning, Rapunzel saw a breathtaking sight: a beautiful kingdom with a castle sitting high above. She headed straight to it!In the town, Rapunzel was drawn to a painting of the King, the Queen, and their baby, who was known as the lost princess.The child had golden hair and green eyes... just like her!lynn rowed Rapunzel out to view the floating lights, which were actually lanterns!Flynn gave Rapunzel her own lantern to send into the night, and she returned the crown.Then the couple gazed into each other's eyes. They were falling in love.Later, Flynn and Rapunzel were separated. Mother Gothel told Rapunzel that Flynn had only wanted the crown.But she realized Mother Gothel was lying! Rapunzel now knew that she was the lost princess!Suddenly, Flynn arrived to rescue Rapunzel! But Mother Gothel hurt him badly. She wanted Rapunzel to stay with her forever.If she did, she'd allow Rapunzel to heal Flynn. But before Rapunzel could act, Flynn cut off her hair, which lost its magic.Without the magic, Mother Gothel quickly aged and turned to dust. Rapunzel was now free, but Flynn was dying."You were my new dream," he whispered. One of Rapunzel's tears fell on Flynn and began to glow... and healed him!nn brought Rapunzel back to the castle. The King and Queen rushed to embrace their lost princess.

That night, the entire kingdom celebrated her return by launching hundreds of lanterns—the lights that had guided her home.

Beauty and the beast

Once upon a time, an Enchantress turned a handsome prince into a terrible beast when she discovered his selfishness.She left behind an enchanted rose. If the prince did not find true love before the last rose petal fell, he would remain a beast forever.In a village nearby, Belle lived with her father. More than anything, Belle wanted an adventure like those she read about in her beloved books.Gaston wanted to marry Belle, but she refused.Belle thought he was a beastly bore, and Gaston didn't understand why she was always reading. "It's not right for a woman to read," he said.Belle's father, Maurice, was an inventor. His latest invention was an automatic woodchopper, which he was taking to a contest at the county fair."You'll win first prize!" Belle declared.On his way to the fair, Maurice got lost in the woods. A pack of wolves chased him to the gates of a nearby castle.

Not sure what he would find inside, Maurice entered the castle grounds cautiously.

Maurice could never have imagined the hideous beast that confronted him.

Thinking Maurice had come to stare at him, the Beast was furious. Without mercy, he locked this unwanted visitor in the dungeon.

When her father's horse came home alone, Belle went in search of her father and found him locked up.Belle begged the Beast for Maurice's freedom. "Take me instead," she offered.The Beast agreed, making her promise to stay in the castle forever!On her first night, Belle met the castle servants. The spell cast by the Enchantress had turned them into enchanted objects!They were funny, friendly, and treated Belle like a special guest.At dinnertime, Belle refused the Beast's invitation to join him, which made him roar with frustration.He was anxious to end the spell - and felt Belle was a sign of hope.

Mrs. Potts, the teapot, and Lumiere, the candelabrum, told him to be patient and, above all, kind.

Later that night, Belle came upon the magic rose the Enchantress had left behind.As Belle reached out to touch it, the Beast appeared and grabbed the precious rose. "Get out!" he yelled.Belle fled the castle on her horse but was attacked by the same wolves that had chased her father.

Belle fled the castle on her horse but was attacked by the same wolves that had chased her father.

Risking his life, the Beast saved Belle. In the days that followed, Belle began to see the goodness in the Beast.

One evening, the Beast again invited Belle to dinner. This time she accepted.

After dinner, the Beast asked Belle to dance. As they whirled around the ballroom, the Beast realized he was in love with Belle.Because of his love, the Beast let Belle return home to see her father.When Gaston heard her speak fondly of the Beast, he grew jealous and stormed the castle.Gaston stabbed the Beast and then was accidentally knocked off the roof.

Belle pulled the Beast to safety. "Please don't leave me," she sobbed. "I love you."

As she spoke, the last rose petal fell. Then a shower of sparks filled the air. The Beast began to transform...

As she spoke, the last rose petal fell. Then a shower of sparks filled the air. The Beast began to transform...

...into a handsome prince!

The enchanted objects were filled with joy as they too turned back into humans and watched their prince and Belle fall in love anew.

Cindrella

Once upon a time, there was a kind girl named Cinderella.All of the animals loved her, especially two mice named Gus and Jaq. They'd do anything for the girl they called Cinderelly.Cinderella lived with her stepmother and her two stepsisters, Anastasia and Drizella.hey were very mean to Cinderella, making her work all day cleaning, sewing, and cooking. She tried her best to make them happy.

Cinderella's stepmother, Lady Tremaine, was cold, cruel, and jealous of Cinderella's charm and beauty.

She enjoyed giving Cinderella extra chores to do, such as bathing her cat, Lucifer.One day, a messenger arrived with a special invitation. There was going to be a royal ball at the palace!The King wanted his son to find a bride. Every young woman in the kingdom was invited—including Cinderella!

The King wanted his son to find a bride. Every young woman in the kingdom was invited—including Cinderella!

Cinderella was very excited about the ball. In the attic, she found a dress that had belonged to her mother.It was a bit old-fashioned, but Cinderella could make it beautiful!Lady Tremaine didn't want Cinderella to go to the ball. She wanted the Prince to meet Anastasia and Drizella. Maybe he would marry one of them!Lady Tremaine kept Cinderella busy with chores that would take her all night to finish.While Cinderella was working, the mice and birds fixed her dress. They added ribbons and beads that the two stepsisters had thrown away.Working together, the animals turned a simple dress into a fabulous gown!Cinderella was overjoyed when she saw the dress. Now she could go to the ball!"Oh, thank you so much!" Cinderella said to Gus, Jaq, and the birds.When the stepsisters saw their old ribbons and beads on Cinderella's dress, they flew into a rage.They ripped the dress and pulled off the beads. Lady Tremaine didn't stop them. Cinderella's dream of going to the ball was through.Cinderella ran away to the garden to cry. Suddenly, her fairy godmother appeared.

Cinderella ran away to the garden to cry. Suddenly, her fairy godmother appeared.

With a wave of her wand, she turned a pumpkin into an elegant coach. Cinderella could now go to the ball, but her dress was still ruined."Bibbidi-bobbidi-boo!" said the Fairy Godmother, waving her wand again. Cinderella was now wearing a beautiful gown and sparkling glass slippers.But all of this came with a warning: When the clock struck midnight, the magic spell would wear off!At the ball, Prince Charming couldn't take his eyes off Cinderella.

The orchestra played, and the Prince began to dance with the wonderful girl whose name he still didn't know. For Cinderella, the night was a dream come true.

Before too long, the clock began to strike midnight. "Good-bye!" Cinderella said, hurrying away."Come back!"

called the Prince. "I don’t even know your name!" As Cinderella fled, one of her glass slippers came off.The Prince sent the Grand Duke to find the girl who fit the glass slipper. Lady Tremaine locked Cinderella in the attic, but Cinderella’s mouse friends freed her.Then Lady Tremaine tripped the Grand Duke, and the glass slipper shattered . . . but Cinderella had the other in her pocket. And it fit!

Cinderella and the Prince were soon married. Everyone rejoiced, including Cinderella’s mouse friends, who wore special outfits to the wedding.Filled with joy, Prince Charming and Cinderella lived happily ever after.

Sleeping beauty

Long ago in a faraway land, a king and his fair queen were blessed with a beautiful baby girl.They named their daughter Aurora, for she filled their lives with light like the dawn.Visitors from throughout the kingdom came to celebrate the birth of the princess, including the three good fairies, who arrived with gifts. fairies, who arrive

Waving their wands, Flora gave the princess the gift of beauty, while Fauna gave her the gift of song.Merryweather was about to bestow her gift when the evil fairy Maleficent appeared in a flash of green fire.She wanted to give the princess something, too - a terrible curse!Before the sun set on her sixteenth birthday, Aurora would prick her finger on the spindle of a spinning wheel and die!

Luckily, Merryweather still had a gift to give. She cast her spell to soften Maleficent's curse.

Now Aurora would not die when she pricked her finger. She would simply fall into a deep slumber, only to be awakened with True Love's Kiss.However, the king and his queen were still very concerned about the safety of their daughter.And so with heavy hearts, they agreed that the three good fairies, disguised as peasant women, would raise the child in secret far away from the castle.Over the years, the child grew into a beautiful young woman who made friends with all of the forest animals.

Her three aunties called her Briar Rose and surrounded her with love. But they never told her the secret of her past.On the day of her sixteenth birthday, Briar Rose still did not know that she was a princess.She spent the morning singing to her friends about how she'd had a glorious dream.In it, she'd met the most wonderful prince. Briar Rose was convinced he was her true love.

Little did Briar Rose know, a prince was passing nearby at that moment. He was Prince Phillip, the very prince that the king and queen had planned for her to marry.Phillip didn't know that Briar Rose was a princess either. But he was so taken with her beautiful song, he hopped off his horse.Phillip emerged from the trees, and as he and Briar Rose sang and danced together, she realized that this man reminded her of the prince in her dreams.She felt as if she'd always known him. Briar Rose was excited for him to meet her aunties, so she invited him to come to the cottage that evening.She knew that she was falling in love.But when Briar Rose returned to the cottage, her aunties told her that they were good fairies and she was a princess.Briar Rose was overcome with sadness. She only wanted to marry the man she had just met, her dream prince.When Aurora arrived at the castle, the three fairies left her alone to mourn. But Maleficent soon appeared to make sure her curse came true.She put Aurora in a trance and led the princess to a spindle hidden high in the castle. There, Aurora pricked her finger and fell into a deep sleep.

When the three fairies found Aurora, they realized that Maleficent's evil curse had come true.They took the sleeping princess to the tower room and then cast a deep sleep over the whole kingdom.

Now they had to find Aurora's true love from the forest so he could give her True Love's Kiss.

It didn't take the three fairies long to recognize that Prince Phillip was the man Aurora had met in the forest - her betrothed was her true love!But he was in Maleficent's dungeon. The fairies freed him and then armed him with the Sword of Truth and the Shield of Virtue.Now he was prepared to fight the evil fairy and save Aurora!

But the evil fairy was not easy to defeat.

Back at the castle, Phillip came face-to-face with Maleficent, who had transformed herself into a giant, fire-breathing dragon.However, with the help of the three good fairies, Phillip was able to send his sword flying swift and sure.With Maleficent gone, Phillip rushed to Aurora's side and bestowed a gentle kiss upon her lips. Aurora's eyes fluttered open - the curse had been broken!When she saw her beloved, the man from the forest, she smiled. Now the prince and princess could live happily ever after.

The frogy prince

As a young girl, Tiana lived in a cozy little house in New Orleans. She and her father loved to cook together.They made the best gumbo in the city!It was their dream to one day open a family restaurant. So one night, Tiana made a wish on the Evening Star that their dream would come true.As Tiana grew up, she never stopped wishing for her own restaurant. But she knew wishing wasn't always enough.She worked hard to make her dream a reality. But that left no time for fun - or for love.One day, Tiana's friend Charlotte asked Tiana to bake her famous beignets. Charlotte was throwing a masquerade ball for a prince named Naveen.With the money from the beignets, Tiana would be one step closer to buying her own restarant!Dressed in a princess costume for the ball, Tiana made one more wish on the Evening Star, still hoping it could make her dream come true.When she was done, a frog spoke to her!It was Prince Naveen! A magic spell had turned him into a frog. Only a kiss from a princess could break the spell, and Naveen thought Tiana was a real pincess.Tiana didn't want to kiss a frog. Then Prince Naveen offered to help her open a restaurant, so she closed her eyes and kissed him.But he didn't turn back into a prince. Instead, she turned into a frog!Frantic, Tiana and Naveen left the party and ended up in a bayou.They met an alligator named Louis who liked to play the trumpet. He knew exactly who could turn them human again: Mama Odie!They met an alligator named Louis who liked to play the trumpet. He knew exactly who could turn them human again: Mama Odie!

As Tiana and Naveen followed Ray the firefly to Mama Odie, they taught each other valuable lessons

Tiana showed Naveen how to work hard for what he wanted, and Naveen taught Tiana that having fun was important. Soon they became great friends.That night, the Evening Star shone bright in the sky. While Louis played a song on his trumpet, Naveen and Tiana danced gracefully together in time with the music.The next day, Tiana and Naveen arrived at Mama Odie's home. She knew all about magic - and human nature.

"You want to be human, but you're blind to what you need!" Mama Odie told them.

Mama Odie used magic to show Tiana and Naveen that Charlotte was to be the Mardi Gras princess for the day.If Charlotte kissed Naveen before midnight, the spell would be broken. They had to hurry home!But by the time Tiana and Naveen returned to town, it was too late. The clock had struck midnight, and they were stuck as frogs forever.But they had each other - and love - which was all they really needed.The two frogs returned to the bayou where they were married among friends. Once wed to Prince Naveen, Tiana became a real princess.This time when she kissed Naveen, not only did he become human - she did, to

Together, Naveen and Tiana opened the restaurant that Tiana had always dreamed about with her father.Tiana finally had everything she wanted - and all that she needed.

Snow white and seven dwarfs

Once upon a time, there was a beautiful princess named Snow White. She was kind and gentle and a friend to all animals.One day, Snow White met a charming prince. As they sang a song of love together, Snow White's evil stepmother, the Queen, watched them.The Queen was so jealous of Snow White's beauty that she ordered her Huntsman to kill the young princess.But the Huntsman couldn't bring himself to hurt Snow White. He told her to run far away so the Queen would never find her.Snow White ran deep into the woods. She was lost and scared but soon found herself in front of a cottage.The princess knocked, but no one was home. She slowly stepped inside.The cottage was a mess! With the help of her forest friends, Snow White cleaned every nook and cranny.The cottage was a mess! With the help of her forest friends, Snow White cleaned every nook and cranny."Maybe whoever lives here will let me stay," said Snow White.Upstairs, Snow White found seven little beds. She thought they belonged to children.Tired from cleaning, Snow White yawned as she curled up on the beds and fell asleep.Meanwhile, the Seven Dwarfs were heading home from a long day of working in a jewel mine. They were anxious to get home to their cottage in the woods.The Seven Dwarfs were surprised when they found a princess inside their home!

When Snow White awoke, she was charmed by the Seven Dwarfs: Dopey, Sneezy, Happy, Grumpy, Doc, Bashful, and Sleepy.The Dwarfs wanted to protect the beautiful princess from the evil queen, so they invited Snow White to live with them.To celebrate, the new friends sang and danced the night away.Back at the castle, the Queen learned that Snow White was still alive.Enraged, she made a magic potion to change her appearance. Her plan was to trick the princess.After the Dwarfs had set off for work the next day, the Queen, disguised as an old peddler woman, offered Snow White a beautiful red apple.Snow White took one bite of the apple and fell into a deep sleep. The Queen had poisoned her!When the Dwarfs came home, they chased the Queen to the top of a stormy mountain. Suddenly, lightning hit the mountain, and the Queen fell, never to be seen again.But Snow White was still in a deep sleep. The Seven Dwarfs kept watch over her day and night.Finally, Snow White's Prince Charming arrived. He had been searching everywhere for the beautiful princess he had sung with so long ago.The Prince awakened Snow White with Love's First Kiss. The spell was broken! Snow White and the Prince returned to the kingdom and lived happily ever after.

Little mermaid

Deep beneath the sea lived a little mermaid named Ariel. She loved exploring her underwater home with her friend flounder but dreamed of living on land as a human.Ariel was always searching for human treasures.When she and Flounder found a strange forked object, they swam to the surface to find Scuttle the seagull."It's a dinglehopper!" he proclaimed.Ariel's father was King Triton, ruler of the sea. He thought humans were dangerous.When he learned that Ariel had been to the surface, he forbade her to ever go again! Then he asked Sebastian the crab to keep an eye on her.But Ariel continued to go to the surface. One night, a terrible storm swept across the sea.Ariel and Flounder watched as a prince fell off a huge ship. "I must save him!" she cried.Ariel pulled Prince Eric to shore and sang to him. Then she swam away.Prince Eric only caught a glimpse of Ariel's face, but he knew he would remember her beautiful voice forever.Desperate to see Prince Eric again, Ariel agreed to give her voice to the evil sea witch Ursula.With bigger plans in mind, Ursula cast a spell......and turned Ariel into a human!But if Prince Eric didn't kiss Ariel by sunset on the third day, she would become a mermaid again.Even worse, she would belong to the sea witch forever!Charmed by her silent beauty, Prince Eric showed Ariel his kingdom.Ariel loved being with the prince in the human world, but the two had not yet kissed.

Worried that Prince Eric was falling in love with Ariel, Ursula transformed herself into the beautiful Vanessa.She was going to make the prince fall in love with her instead.Disguised as Vanessa and using Ariel's voice, the sea witch cast a spell on Prince Eric. He thought he was in love.He was going to marry Vanessa! Ariel had lost her true love.Just before sunset on the third day, Scuttle discovered that Vanessa was Ursula in disguise. He hurried to warn Ariel.As Sebastian went to find King Triton, Ariel and Flounder raced to catch Prince Eric's ship.As Sebastian went to find King Triton, Ariel and Flounder raced to catch Prince Eric's ship.Released from Ursula's spell, Prince Eric realized that Ariel was the one he truly loved. But it was too late.

The sun went down before Ariel and the prince could kiss. She was a mermaid once more, and she belonged to Ursula.To save his daughter, King Triton gave Ursula his great powers and became her prisoner. "Now I am the ruler of all the ocean!" shouted Ursula.As Ursula grew in size and towered above the sea, Prince Eric jumped aboard an old ship.He steered its jagged bow through Ursula's heart. With a howl, the sea witch disappeared in the waves.With Ursula gone, King Triton regained his powers. Seeing Ariel's love for Prince Eric, the king granted her wish: She became human!Ariel and Prince Eric married and lived happily in a castle by the sea.

9 798885 033534

Printed by Libri Plureos GmbH in Hamburg, Germany